D1472620

MULTICULTURAL
LITERATURE

A READER'S GUIDE TO
ZORA NEALE HURSTON'S

Their Eyes Were Watching God

LAURA BASKES LITWIN

Enslow Publishers, Inc.
40 Industrial Road
Box 398
Berkeley Heights, NJ 07922
USA

http://www.enslow.com

Library of Congress Cataloging-in-Publication Data

Litwin, Laura Baskes.

A reader's guide to Zora Neale Hurston's Their eyes were watching god / Laura Baskes Litwin.

p. cm. — (Multicultural literature)

Includes bibliographical references (p.) and index.

Summary: "An introduction to Zora Neale Hurston's novel Their eyes were watching God for high school students, which includes biographical background on the author, explanations of various literary devices and techniques, and literary criticism for the novice reader"—Provided by publisher.

ISBN-13: 978-0-7660-3164-7

ISBN-10: 0-7660-3164-0

1. Hurston, Zora Neale. Their eyes were watching God—Juvenile literature. 2. African American women in literature. I. Title.

PS3515.U789T536 2010

813'.52—dc22

2008038524

Printed in the United States of America

112009 Lake Book Manufacturing, Inc., Melrose Park, IL

10 9 8 7 6 5 4 3 2 1

To Our Readers:

We have done our best to make sure all Internet addresses in this book were active and appropriate when we went to press. However, the author and publisher have no control over and assume no liability for the material available on those Internet sites or on other Web sites they may link to. Any comments or suggestions can be sent by e-mail to comments@enslow.com or to the address on the back cover.

♻ Enslow Publishers, Inc., is committed to printing our books on recycled paper. The paper in every book contains 10% to 30% post-consumer waste (PCW). The cover board on the outside of each book contains 100% PCW. Our goal is to do our part to help young people and the environment too!

Photos and Illustrations: Courtesy of the State Archives of Florida, pp. 7, 9; General Research Division, The New York Public Library, Astor, Lenox and Tilden Foundations, p. 93; Library of Congress, Prints and Photographs Division, Carl Van Vechten Collection, pp. 4; Library of Congress, Prints and Photographs Division, Lomax Collection, pp. 53, 105; Library of Congress, Prints and Photographs Division, p. 12; The Granger Collection, New York, p. 50; Vivian Zink/ © ABC/ Everett Collection, Inc., pp. 33, 37.

Cover Illustration: Vivian Zink/ © ABC/ Everett Collection, Inc.

Contents

Zora Neale Hurston

CHAPTER 1

About the Author

In the summer of 1973, ten years before she would win a Pulitzer Prize and the National Book award for her novel The Color Purple, *author Alice Walker stood in an old cemetery in central Florida. Though she was waist-deep in buggy weeds and fearful of the snakes in the grasses at her feet, Walker was determined to find a certain grave.*

Alice Walker's literary hero was buried in this cemetery: Zora Neale Hurston, of whose master-work, *Their Eyes Were Watching God*, Walker would write simply, but in italics, *"There is no book more important to me than this one."*[1]

Walker's mission was further complicated by the fact that Hurston's grave had no marker. When Zora Neale Hurston died in 1960, she was penniless. None of her books were in print, and she had not published a novel in a dozen years. This dire situation was not a new one for Hurston. She had faced poverty her entire life. In her last years, she was forced to take a job as a maid in order to pay her bills.

Zora Neale Hurston was born in 1891, though she would subtract ten years from her true age for all of her adulthood, leaving biographers uncertain of her actual birth date for many years. She was raised in a unique Florida town called Eatonville, the first incorporated, all-African-American town in the United States. In her autobiography, Hurston would describe her hometown as "a pure Negro town—charter, mayor, council, town marshal and all."[2]

Zora Neale Hurston (1891–1960), author and anthropologist. It would take more than a decade after her death for her book *Their Eyes Were Watching God* and her life to gain the public's interest.

In Eatonville, unlike almost any other place in America at the time, blacks were free from white authority and the community thrived. The town's traditions would play an essential role in all of Hurston's writings. She understood that the culture in which she had grown up was unusual in the close attention paid to its heritage. The people of Eatonville were proud of their traditions and spent time recounting them, often while sitting on the front porch of the town's general store.

Hurston's father, John, the son of sharecroppers, was a minister and strict disciplinarian of his eight children. Zora was much closer to her mother, Lucy, an affectionate and nurturing woman who encouraged her daughter's creative spirit. She died when Zora was just thirteen. When John Hurston remarried a year later, he sent his older children to boarding school in Jacksonville, Florida.

Jacksonville was not Eatonville. For the first time in her life, Zora was exposed to racism and the ugly segregation of Jim Crow laws. "Jacksonville made me know I was a little colored girl," she would

Pastor John Hurston, Zora Neale Hurston's father.

write later.[3] The next period of her life was a difficult one. For eight years, beginning at age sixteen,
Hurston attended school irregularly and worked
several different jobs, including as a domestic in
various households.

In her mid-twenties she was finally able to return to school full-time. It was at this time that she began to claim that she was ten years younger than she actually was. She finished high school and began college at Howard University in Washington, D.C., the largest and most prominent African-American university in the country.

In 1925 Hurston moved to New York City and transferred to Barnard College on a full scholarship. The only African-American student at the school, Hurston attracted the attention of professor and renowned anthropologist Franz Boas. And his interest was for reasons other than the mere fact of her color.

Boas was impressed by Hurston's intelligence and initiative. Under his tutelage, she began collecting the stories, songs, and customs of African Americans in the Deep South. This work was pioneering. Anthropologists had never before studied African-American folklore.

Hurston began her folklore collecting in her hometown of Eatonville, but soon journeyed far beyond Florida. A bold and independent woman, she traveled alone throughout the rural South, a loaded pistol in her purse for protection. To observe indigenous social and religious rituals, she ventured to remote jungles on Caribbean islands and in Central America.

Her work in anthropology placed her among the top scholars in the field. Her book on African-American folklore, *Mules and Men,* is still considered one of the best on the subject. Yet Zora Neale Hurston always considered herself a writer first and a folklorist second.

It was a winning prize in a writing contest that first brought her to New York City in 1925. In Harlem, she met Langston Hughes, Countee Cullen, and Wallace Thurman, among others. Her life as a serious writer had begun. While Hurston was very much a part of the artistic community in

Hurston plays a Haitian mama drum, also known as a hountar. This photograph was taken in 1937 while she was in the Caribbean studying the local customs.

the 1920s known as the Harlem Renaissance, her most important book was not written until the decade following.

In 1936 the prestigious Guggenheim Foundation awarded Hurston a yearlong grant to study the folklore customs of blacks in the West Indies. She went first to Jamaica, and then on to Haiti, where she observed séances and animal sacrifices performed as part of voodoo rituals.

It was during this visit to Haiti, in a mere seven weeks, that Hurston wrote *Their Eyes Were Watching God.* The book is a heated tale of love and passion. One of the reasons she was able to write it as quickly as she did was that the story drew directly from her own life.

In the months immediately preceding her trip to the Caribbean, Hurston had been involved with a man named Percival McGuire Punter. Twenty years younger than Hurston, handsome and intelligent, Punter was, in her words, "the real love affair of my life."[4] Still, when he insisted Hurston give up her career and take care of him, she ended the relationship. She would write years later, "I really wanted to do anything he wanted me to do, but that one thing I could not do."[5]

The Guggenheim-financed trip came at the right time for Hurston. To escape her hurt feelings, she immersed herself in work. The raw, tangled ends of the failed romance made their way into the novel. The central characters of *Their Eyes Were Watching God,* Janie and Tea Cake, are in many respects fictional versions of Hurston and Punter.

During her whole career, Zora Neale Hurston would publish seven books, including an autobiography, two books on folklore, and four novels, and more than fifty shorter pieces. *Their Eyes Were Watching God* is widely considered her greatest work and now is taught in high schools and universities.

Alice Walker did finally locate Hurston's grave and had a headstone made to honor the writer who had most inspired her. The simple epitaph reads: Zora Neale Hurston: A Genius of the South.[6] After nearly four decades of neglect, Zora Neale Hurston would posthumously become among the most heralded of African-American writers.

CHAPTER 2

Plot Summary and Analysis

Zora Neale Hurston's *Their Eyes Were Watching God* is the tale of Janie Crawford, a resourceful and independent African-American woman. The novel opens with Janie's return home following a two-year absence. Aware that the nosy townspeople are eager for gossip—"their ears full of hope"[1]—Janie relates the details of her journey to her best friend, Pheoby Watson.

When Janie first appears, neighbors cluck their tongues, assuming the worst about her circumstances. When last seen, Janie wore a silk dress. Clad now in denim overalls, they speculate that her husband has taken her money and left her for a younger woman.

With a welcoming casserole in hand, Pheoby wastes no time making her way to Janie's back porch. Pheoby distinguishes herself from the town gossips. She is a true friend and confidante. Janie chooses to tell her story to Pheoby with the tacit understanding that her friend can be trusted when repeating it to the others.

Janie Crawford's story is told in a single, extended flashback. Hurston structures the novel with a frame, a literary device used to give order to a long or complicated sequence of events. *Their Eyes Were Watching God* begins and ends with Janie and Pheoby sitting together on Janie's back porch. The novel spans nearly four decades of Janie's life but is "framed" by a single evening's visit between two friends.

While the framing device sets up the novel as her own story, Janie does not tell it in the first person. Instead, a separate narrative voice is used for most of the book. Exactly who speaks as this omniscient narrator is not entirely clear. One reviewer has suggested that it is "Janie's consciousness" talking.[2] Noted African-American scholar Henry Louis Gates, Jr., maintains that the third-person narrator speaks both for Janie and the community as a whole.[3] This narrator allows Janie's three husbands, her Nanny, the porch sitters, and others to speak in different voices, creating a kind of chorus spinning the larger tale of Janie's life.

Janie begins her narrative with some family background. She describes her youth, growing up with her Nanny, who helped raise several white children as well. Janie reveals she had believed she too was white until she was six years old and saw a photograph of herself. This anecdote mirrors events in Hurston's own life. Until she left Eatonville for school, Hurston's color was of little consequence. In Jacksonville, though, the segregated bathrooms and streetcars were constant reminders that some people considered her a second-class citizen.

Nanny, Janie's grandmother, is determined to make a better life for her. She tells her granddaughter, "Ah been waitin' a long time, Janie, but nothin' Ah been through ain't too much if you just take a stand on high ground lak Ah dreamed."[4]

For Nanny, what guarantees a better life begins with the protection of a man. When she discovers sixteen-year-old Janie kissing a neighborhood boy, Nanny quickly arranges a marriage to Logan Killicks, an older man. He looks "like some old skullhead in the graveyard,"[5] but is also the owner of a house and a mule on sixty acres.

Nanny sees the kissing of a local boy, the "shiftless"[6] Johnny Taylor, as a threat to Janie's future. Nanny has endured slavery, her own rape by a white master, and her daughter's rape by a schoolteacher, which resulted in Janie's birth. She is determined to arrange a better life for Janie. While Logan Killicks is unappealing, it is understandable why Nanny views his financial stability as a benefit.

Yet Logan Killicks offers Janie little but security. He expects her to work long, hard days in the potato fields. Janie feels isolated and sad, describing her new home as "a lonesome place like a stump in the middle of the woods."[7] The teenager craves the excitement of love, confiding to her grandmother, "Ah wants to want him sometime."[8] Crushed by the loveless marriage, the naïve girl grows up quickly. "She knew now that marriage did not make love. Janie's first dream was dead, so she became a woman."[9]

Soon after becoming a woman, Janie meets Joe Starks, a sophisticated, smooth-talking, and self-assured sort, and runs off with him. The two marry en route to Eatonville, Florida, where Joe "aimed tuh be uh big voice"[10] and is elected mayor. He buys land and sets up the town post office and general store.

Unhappily for Janie, however, Joe expects her to act like "Mrs. Mayor" and be superior to her neighbors. "She must look on herself as the bell-cow, the other women were the gang."[11] Similarly, as the mayor's wife, the residents of Eatonville keep their distance from her, believing "she slept with authority and so she was part of it in the town mind."[12] As she had been in her first marriage, Janie finds herself lonely in her second.

The couple's relationship continues to deteriorate, reaching a low point when Joe slaps Janie simply for what to him was a poorly cooked dinner. A few days later he humiliates her in front of a group at the store. Then, Janie replies with harsh words of her own.

Joe becomes ill and blames Janie. As he weakens, she tries to discuss their marital difficulties, but he is uninterested and unapologetic. When Joe Starks dies, Janie is left financially independent. Outwardly, she feigns sorrow and respect for her dead husband, but secretly she relishes her freedom.

After two failed marriages, Janie is certain that her grandmother's "dream of what a woman oughta be and to do"[13] is a false one. Then Vergible "Tea Cake" Woods saunters into the general store one afternoon. To Janie, it "seemed as if she had known him all her life."[14]

Tea Cake, much younger than Janie, is a free spirit and a gambler. He is the first man she has known who treats her as a valued individual and cares about her happiness. He helps her in the store and he cooks for her. Tea Cake teaches Janie to play checkers, shoot a gun, and drive a car, and he takes her fishing at midnight on a whim.

Janie and Tea Cake marry and move south to the Everglades. They find jobs together as bean pickers in the swampy marshes known as "the muck."[15] Their house is a simple shack but also a joyful, loving home of equals. In the evenings, the other migrant workers gather there for parties with music, dancing, and gambling.

Overnight, the couple's contented existence is wrecked by a hurricane. While attempting to save Janie's life in the raging storm, Tea Cake is bitten by a rabid dog. When the weather clears, he is forced by white lawmen to act as a gravedigger and to separate the corpses by race. Whites will receive coffins while blacks will be buried in a mass grave.

As the rabies ravages his body, Tea Cake goes mad and tries to shoot Janie. In self-defense, she shoots and kills him. Janie is charged with murder and goes to trial. In the courtroom, an all-white jury acquits her. Following an elaborate funeral for Tea Cake, Janie returns to Eatonville to tell her story to Pheoby.

CHAPTER 3

Character Study: Janie Crawford

Janie Crawford is the storyteller of *Their Eyes Were Watching God.* Hers is the central, overarching voice of the novel. While Janie's story is unique, it is recognizable as well for its universal truths. Houston A. Baker, Jr., a professor at Vanderbilt University, has compared Janie to "a singer who . . . recapitulates the blues experience of all black women."[1]

The reader is first introduced to Janie as she returns home, the prying focus of a gossiping community. Janie's neighbors are eager to know what has happened to the feisty forty-year-old woman who, when last seen, was skipping town to marry a twenty-five-year-old drifter.

Wagging tongues assume the worst: Janie Crawford left Eatonville in a blue silk wedding dress and has come back in overalls. But careful eyes can see that Janie is in no distress. After she and her best friend, Pheoby, finish their casserole dinner, they settle in comfortably on the porch for a good long talk.

Janie Crawford is a woman in full control. This had not always been the case. In the years spanned by the novel, Janie matures from a naïve girl into a strong and independent adult. She is raised by her Nanny, a former slave who wants for her granddaughter precisely that which was denied to her, all "whut a woman oughta be and to do."[2] For Janie's grandmother, slavery is an actual memory and a defining aspect of her later life.

Nanny works for a white family and Janie is six years old before she sees a photograph and realizes that she herself is black. This self-discovery is the first in a string of many others to follow.

At sixteen, Janie's sexual awakening is cut short by her protective grandmother. As the novel's narrator describes succinctly, when Nanny catches Janie kissing a boy, "that was the end of her childhood."[3] A victim herself of sexual oppression, Nanny wants to safeguard Janie at all costs. Nanny believes that marriage—never even an option for her—is a woman's best defense against sexual abuse.

Nanny thinks marriage will protect the African-American woman from her traditional fate as "mule uh de world."[4] She envisions a better existence for Janie, removed from the drudgery that has characterized her own life. To this end, she arranges for Janie to marry the financially secure Logan Killicks.

Logan Killicks is sixty and ugly and while he fulfills Nanny's dreams, he does the opposite for Janie. The teenager longs for love "but Janie didn't know how to tell Nanny that."[5] The marriage proves to be little more than a business partnership. When

Logan chides her for failing to keep up her end of the plow, Janie leaves him for Joe Starks.

At first glance, Joe appears to satisfy both Nanny's concerns and Janie's needs. He has money, ambition, and an oversized personality. Joe dazzles Janie, but then, just as quickly, he puts a stranglehold on her life.

Joe considers Janie a mere possession, an accessory to his standing in the community. Even worse, he demands total submission from her. He insists she hide her long, luxurious hair under a scarf and keep all thoughts to herself in public. When Janie is encouraged to give a speech, Joe belittles her, announcing to the assembled group, "mah wife don't know nothin' 'bout no speech-makin'."[6]

Over time, Janie is worn down by this forced humility, "so gradually, she pressed her teeth together and learned to hush."[7] In many ways, Janie endures a second marriage as loveless and confining as her first. Yet, Janie never allows her spirit to be crushed completely.

Outwardly, she seems to yield. In her deepest self, however, she "was saving up feelings for some man she had never seen."[8] When Joe is dying from kidney failure, Janie confronts him with the angry feelings she had previously suppressed. She tells him, "Mah own mind had tuh be squeezed and crowded out tuh make room for yours in me."[9]

In the weeks immediately following Joe's death, Janie realizes that while Nanny may have had her best interests at heart, the focus on material things has cheated Janie of years of freedom. Logan Killicks and Joe Starks may have provided security, but that would never be enough for Janie.

When Vergible "Tea Cake" Woods saunters into her store, Janie understands that she needs more than financial stability to be happy. With Tea Cake, Janie's "soul crawled out from its hiding place,"[10] and her true self emerges. Janie now finds real love—both for a man and, more important, for herself.

Janie's growth comes *alongside* Tea Cake but not *through* him. From the beginning, Janie and Tea Cake are equals. For the first time, Janie finds meaning in a passionate, loving relationship, with no material or social strings attached. In addition to being Tea Cake's partner, Janie becomes an integral member of the community too.

The couple's home becomes the nightly meeting place for their fellow workers. Unlike Joe Starks, Tea Cake supports Janie's right to self-expression and "she got so she could tell big stories herself."[11]

Given the nature of her love for Tea Cake, picking beans with him feels almost like play to Janie. Both Nanny and Joe Starks would have believed this to be beneath her, but Janie finally finds true happiness in this life. Tea Cake shows Janie the glory of a life apart from financial security and the social restrictions that accompany it. In choosing love and equal partnership over material concerns, Janie becomes a person of substance.

While Janie does finally find fulfillment in her third marriage, Tea Cake falls short of being a perfect spouse. One day he hits Janie, a brutality made worse by the reactions of his admiring friends. His best pal, Sop-de-Bottom, exclaims, "wouldn't Ah love tuh whip uh tender woman lak Janie!"[12] Surprisingly, Hurston never provides the reader with Janie's response to the beating. Because Janie resists male control throughout the novel, some critics have questioned her curious silence in this instance. Likewise, when she is on trial for Tea Cake's murder and her freedom is at stake, Janie barely speaks in the courtroom. Her story instead is related to the jury by men who barely know her.

Renowned feminist critic and essayist Mary Helen Washington writes, "Hurston was indeed ambivalent about giving a powerful voice to a woman like Janie who is already in rebellion against male authority and against the roles prescribed for women in a male-dominated society."[13]

When the rabies overtakes Tea Cake and he tries to kill her, Janie must shoot him in self-defense. But despite these heartrending events, the novel's conclusion is not a tragic one. Tea Cake's death represents something larger. It shows her that she can survive without him.

In fact, by the end of the book, Janie feels so strong that she views herself as a controlling influence in Tea Cake's continued existence. "Of course he wasn't dead," she thinks to herself. "He could never be dead until she herself had finished feeling and thinking."[14] The novel's final passage demonstrates the extent of Janie's growth and self-realization. "Here was peace. She pulled in her horizon like a great fish-net. Pulled it from around the waist of the world and draped it over her shoulder. So much of life in its meshes! She called in her soul to come and see."[15]

CHAPTER 4

Character Studies: Janie Crawford's Men

Hoping to spare her granddaughter the difficult fate of many African-American women of the time, Nanny arranges Janie's first marriage. The well-meaning effort is doomed from the start. Logan Killicks is a thoroughly unattractive, much older man. As Janie describes him, "His belly is too big . . . and his toe-nails look lak mule foots."[1] A successful farmer, his idea of a wife is a fellow worker in the fields.

Sixteen-year-old Janie makes neither a good farmhand nor a happy wife. She wants "things sweet wid mah marriage,"[2] and Logan fails to consider the desires of a young girl.

He is strictly a provider, not a lover. From his perspective, a good husband is one who buys his wife a second mule to help with the plowing. Janie realizes that the marriage will never work for her: "The familiar people and things had failed her so she hung over the gate and looked up the road towards way off."[3]

What Janie finds coming down that road is another man. He tells her she is meant not to labor in the potato fields but to sit "on de front porch and rock and fan yo'self."[4] These are enticing words for the teenager and she runs off with the glib and ambitious Joe Starks.

Joe provides Janie with the means to escape her unhappy marriage. He is on his way to Eatonville, Florida, the African-American town where his money and powers of persuasion will buy him property and get him elected mayor. After his election, he builds himself a large house that resembles a plantation mansion.

Joe is a stylish dresser with the protruding stomach of a man who has never had to go hungry. He smokes a cigar, symbolic of his position as town leader. His self-confidence borders on arrogance. He appears to Janie at first as a man who "spoke for change and chance,"[5] but turns quickly into a stifling boss with "uh throne in de seat of his pants."[6] As one of Joe's constituents in the

Their Eyes Were Watching God was adapted into a television movie in 2005. Halle Berry starred as Janie Crawford. Ruben Santiago-Hudson played Joe Starks.

town notes, "He loves obedience out of everybody under de sound of his voice."[7]

From the beginning, Janie is little more than a token of Joe's stature in the town, his "pretty doll-baby."[8] Joe sees Janie as his possession, no different from the general store or the post office or the land that he owns. He isolates his wife from the larger community, refusing to permit her even to take part in everyday conversation. One day she reacts to Joe's insults with some strong ones of her own, publicly questioning his manhood.

Following Janie's verbal attack on him, Joe becomes ill with a kidney condition from which he will not recover. On his deathbed, Janie tells him: "All dis bowin' down, all dis obedience under yo' voice—dat ain't whut Ah rushed off down de road tuh find out about you."[9]

While Janie finally stands up to Joe, she never finds true happiness with him. That kind of joy emerges with her next husband. Vergible "Tea Cake"

Woods is a young man who radiates confidence. In his mid-twenties, he is already comfortable with who he is and where he fits in the world. Unlike Logan Killicks or Joe Starks, he has no attachment to the usual symbols of power—money and status—and neither does he seem to need or even want them. Tea Cake's power comes from within, from his ease with himself.

Tea Cake appears one day in Janie's store, seemingly out of nowhere. Despite an immediate physical attraction, Janie frets about his relative youth and thinks he is "probably the kind of man who lived with various women but never married."[10] Yet in the following weeks, Tea Cake demonstrates a kindness and a lightheartedness that thoroughly charms her.

What separates Tea Cake from the previous men in Janie's life is that he requires only that she be herself. By doing this, he encourages her self-confidence, which has suffered in earlier relationships. For the first time in her life, Janie falls in love.

Tea Cake is the antithesis of Joe Starks. He does not need to stifle Janie in order to prove his own worth. He urges her to speak her mind, to "have de nerve to say whut you mean."[11] With Tea Cake, Janie "could listen and laugh and . . . tell big stories herself."[12]

From the beginning, Tea Cake views Janie as an individual. The day they meet he teaches her to play checkers, a game Joe had told her "wuz too heavy fuh mah brains."[13] Tea Cake's simple gesture uncorks emotions Janie had kept bottled up. She "found herself glowing inside. Somebody wanted her to play. Somebody thought it natural for her to play."[14]

Over the next weeks, Tea Cake woos Janie. He takes her fishing in the moonlight and to the big church picnic. He plays the guitar for her, and he teaches her how to use a gun. What is more, he

Janie finds true love with Tea Cake Woods (played by Michael Ealy).

is not afraid of letting her know that he loves her, that she holds "de keys to de kingdom."[15]

After marrying, the couple moves to Jacksonville, where Janie is introduced to Tea Cake's friends. Like him, they are seasonal farm-workers, gamblers, and musicians. Tea Cake worries Janie "ain't usetuh folks lat dat."[16] But she warms to the community at once and their home becomes the social center after work.

Although he is not a male chauvinist like Joe Starks, Tea Cake is not the perfect man, as an episode of violence shows. In a fit of jealousy, he hits Janie one day in order to "show her he was boss."[17] While Janie does not appear to respond to the beating, it is perhaps not a coincidence that soon after her marriage comes to an end.

After this public humiliation, Janie kills Tea Cake in self-defense. She seems to forgive him in the days immediately following the beating, but her inner self begins to rebel. As much as she loves Tea Cake, Janie chooses to kill him in order to live herself.

CHAPTER 5

Character Studies: Minor Characters

After Janie Crawford and the three men she marries—Logan Killicks, Joe Starks, and Vergible "Tea Cake" Woods—a cast of minor characters play important roles in the novel.

Janie's grandmother is referred to by no name other than Nanny. An ex-slave, she is zealous in her desire to protect Janie from a life of servitude. Her aspirations for Janie, however, stop short at material security. Never having experienced love or respect in a relationship with a man, Nanny fails to understand that her granddaughter will want and seek these. When Nanny dies, Janie feels alone and ultimately angry at Nanny's attempt to "choke her"[1] in the name of security.

In fact, Nanny wants more than mere material possessions for Janie. She hopes for personal autonomy for her granddaughter as well. Nanny tells Janie, "Ah wanted to preach a great sermon about colored women sittin' on high, but there wasn't no pulpit for me . . . Ah been waitin a long time, Janie, but nothin' Ah been through ain't too much if you just take a stance on high ground lak ah dreamed."[2]

By connecting material security with self-empowerment, Nanny's advice is inadequate for Janie. But it is understandable in the context of her own slave memories. "Ah was born back due in slavery so it wasn't for me to fulfill my dreams of whut a woman oughta be and to do . . . but nothing can't stop you from wishin'."[3]

In Greek mythology, Phoebe is the goddess of wise counsel and thoughtful replies. In *Their Eyes Were Watching God,* Pheoby Watson plays this same part for Janie Crawford. Pheoby is Janie's best friend and closest confidante. It is to her that Janie narrates the story of her life. In contrast to the women in town who condemn Janie on sight, Pheoby is a loyal companion. She demonstrates none of the petty jealousies that characterize the others. She is an encouraging and careful listener whom Janie trusts to fairly relate her story to the community At the end of the novel, Pheoby promises to protect Janie's reputation. What is more, she tells Janie that her story has transformed her. In Pheoby's words, "Ah done growed ten feet higher from jus' listen' tuh you, Janie."[4]

Sam Watson is Pheoby's husband. He enjoys a good joke and the give-and-take of daily conversation. While he is a vocal member of the porch-sitting chorus, his is a voice of tolerance. Like his wife, Sam defends Janie against Eatonville's scorn. The residents of Eatonville are a church-going, industrious group. While they may be defined as working class, they aspire to the values of the middle class, striving for material wealth and social respectability. After putting in a full day in the fields, at the post office, or at the general store, they congregate for a bit of gossip—the men on Joe Starks' porch, the women at their homes.

The Eatonville porch-sitters have sharp tongues and often sit in judgment of one another. When Janie returns home after Tea Cake's funeral, she is fully aware of the envy and resentment of her neighbors. These women are meant to appear intimidating and have proper, conservative names such as Pearl Stone and Mrs. Sumpkins.

With the exceptions of Pheoby and Sam Watson, the porch-sitters are not significant characters as individuals. Instead, they exist as a group and function as a type of chorus. Their dialogue serves as a running commentary, scrutinizing the actions of the main characters.

Unlike the porch-sitters from Eatonville with their standard names and titles, the characters on the muck where Janie works with Tea Cake are defined by colorful nicknames that add cultural texture to the novel. Some names are based on physical traits and others on personality. Each name is important as much for what it sounds like when spoken aloud, as when read.

The muck laborers—Sop-de-Bottom, Coodemay, Motor Boat, Bootyny, and Stew Beef, among others—are named both to differentiate each of them as vital members of an established community, as well as to connect them to that community as a whole.

Mrs. Turner is the exception to this carefree group, as is evidenced by her established name and title. Her prejudice against her fellow African Americans with darker skin color reveals the extent of racism within the black community. Mrs. Turner befriends Janie simply because she admires her caramel-colored skin tone and long straight hair.

As the owner of the local restaurant on the muck, Mrs. Turner depends on the workers' patronage. When Tea Cake and his friends have had enough of her racist attitudes, they stage a brawl and destroy her restaurant.

The itinerant workers exist from hand-to-mouth, never worrying about saving money or what the future will bring. To their minds, owning a house or buying land is an ambition of a different class of people altogether. The laborers play as hard as they work:

> All night long the jooks clanged and clamored.
> Pianos living three lifetimes in one. Blues made
> and used right on the spot. Dancing, fighting,
> singing, crying, laughing, winning and losing
> love every hour.[5]

This dancing, gambling, and fighting has as much a place on the muck as it fails to have in staid Eatonville. While the muck workers live on the edge and move frequently, they still manage to forge a lively and caring community.

CHAPTER 6

Folklore and Language

I was glad when somebody told me, "You may go and collect Negro folklore." In a way it would not be a new experience for me. When I pitched headforemost into the world I landed in the crib of negroism. From the earliest rocking of my cradle, I had known about the capers Brer Rabbit is apt to cut and what the Squinch Owl says from the house top. But it was fitting me like a tight chemise. I couldn't see it for wearing it. It was only when I was off in college, away from my native surroundings, that I could see myself like somebody else and stand off and look at my garment. Then I had to have the spy-glass of Anthropology to look through at that.[1]

So begins Zora Neale Hurston's treasury of African-American folklore, *Mules and Men*. Published in 1935, it is still considered one of the very best books on the subject. The folk traditions expressed in *Their Eyes Were Watching God* were first explored by Hurston in *Mules and Men*.

How Zora Neale Hurston came to become an esteemed academic scholar of the culture in which she was raised is a story of its own. In 1925, Hurston entered Barnard College as the women's school's only African-American student. Barnard is part of Columbia University, an Ivy League school, located on the Upper West Side of Manhattan.

Hurston was less concerned with breaking the color line at Barnard than she was with finding the money to pay tuition. She received scholarships and worked two jobs outside of school, but funds were always scarce.

Literature and composition remained her primary interests until a faculty adviser suggested a course in anthropology, the study of human culture. The anthropology department at Columbia, where Barnard students were permitted to take classes, was world renowned. Its reputation came in large part from the acclaim given to the work of one professor, Franz Boas.

Boas was an expert in the area of anthropology called cultural relativism. This field is based on the premise that every race has its own unique characteristics worthy of study. Hurston quickly proved herself to be one of Boas's finest students, and he arranged a six-month research fellowship for her.

The research grant money came from the foundation of Carter G. Woodson, the most important African-American historian in the country. Hurston was assigned the task of collecting the songs, stories, and customs of African Americans in the southern United States.

Since the time of slavery, African Americans had attached great value to their oral tradition. For one thing, laws in many slave-holding states had made it illegal for slaves or even freed blacks to learn to read. Whites feared literacy might ease the way for blacks to organize, prompting an uprising.

But another essential reason the act of story-telling was important to enslaved African Americans was that it permitted them a sense of themselves as vital human beings. The folktales, spirituals, and jokes, shared while doing backbreaking work in the cotton fields, helped to ease their terrible circumstances and to affirm their culture.

African-American folklore had received no scholarly attention before this time, and Hurston appeared to be an ideal researcher. As an African American raised in the Deep South, she understood its traditions. Yet, Hurston soon discovered that collecting folklore was no easy task. What she had learned from her college textbooks did not help much out in the field, and her university degree got her nowhere with ordinary folk.

"The glamour of Barnard College was still upon me," she wrote some time after. "I dwelt in marble halls. I knew where the material was all right. But, I went around asking, in carefully accented Barnardese, 'Pardon me, but do you know any folk tales or folk songs?'"[2]

A few months later, Hurston had gotten the knack of things. In an old car she nicknamed Sassy Susie, she drove the unpaved back roads of the rural South, understanding that her best chance at finding authentic material was to go "where there are the least outside influences and these people, being usually under-privileged, are the shyest."[3]

In the summer of 1927, Hurston's close friend Langston Hughes, a poet from Harlem, joined her in Mobile, Alabama. He was very interested in the different dialects and language patterns of the rural South. Often, in order to help ease the comfort

Zora Neale Hurston (right) stands with Harlem Renaissance writers Langston Hughes (center) and Jessie Redmon Fauset (left) beside a statue of influential educator Booker T. Washington in Alabama, 1927.

level of the people from whom she was collecting folklore, Hurston would read Hughes' poetry aloud and pass out refreshments.

Hurston dutifully copied all she heard in dozens of notebooks, but her skills at collecting went far beyond merely recording. Because she had grown up hearing the same kinds of colorful idioms and stories, Hurston was able to faithfully recreate the texture and rhythm of the language, on top of transcribing it. Her ear was fine-tuned for this work.

When her assignments for Franz Boas ended, Hurston continued her own research, often under extremely dangerous circumstances. She posed as a bootlegger-on-the-run in a lumber camp in Florida and nearly was knifed. Studying Caribbean music in the Bahamas, she survived a fierce five-day hurricane. A voodoo doctor in Haiti tried to poison her.

Yet, for all her bold traveling, it was Hurston's close-knit hometown of Eatonville, Florida, that would provide the richest material for her folklore collection. From early childhood, Hurston heard the voices that would shape her stories.

Like the residents of most small towns, the men and women of Eatonville shared gossip and other concerns on a daily basis. Most often, they gathered to talk on the front porch of Joe Clark's general store.

Joe Clark was one of Eatonville's original settlers and its second mayor. (He serves as the model for Joe Starks in the novel.) On Clark's porch, the young Hurston listened to the folktales that had roots deep in her people's culture and learned firsthand the value of storytelling.

In many respects, Hurston meant *Their Eyes Were Watching God* to be read as one very long porch tale. Janie tells her story to Pheoby while the two sit together on Janie's back porch. The narration is revealed at the same time to the reader listening in like an invisible eavesdropper.

The novel tracks many years of Janie's life, "framed" in the single evening's conversation.

Zora Neale Hurston observes a folk musician during a 1935 recording expedition to her hometown of Eatonville, Florida.

The frame is commonly used as a structuring device in storytelling and folklore. Pheoby is supposed to retell Janie's story to the community at large. It is understood that her retelling will echo Janie's in a general way, but also will have slight differences as well. It will be reconstructed by a second speaker: That is the nature of storytelling.

Janie's long journey itself is reminiscent of many a folktale. Like other folktale heroines, she leaves home, faces a slew of tough challenges, and returns enlightened and triumphant. As in the Brer Rabbit stories, Hurston's characters speak in a specific, rich, idiomatic language. The southern African-American dialect Hurston employs is never bogged down by standard grammar or a concern with sounding refined. Hurston draws on the conversations of her youth, cherishing the language of her culture.

This dialect may appear confusing to some readers at first reading. Vowels are mixed up—"get" becomes "git" and "I" is always "Ah." "Ain't" is used everywhere. The double negative, such as "Naw indeed, we can't do nothin',"[4] works to strengthen the speaker's emphasis.

As an anthropologist and a writer, Hurston believed that the jokes, stories, and songs she witnessed needed to be reported exactly as she had heard them. Anything less would misrepresent or dilute their distinctive sound. The author's careful use of Eatonville's regional speech animates her characters while serving, at the same time, to make them more believable. Janie, Joe, Tea Cake, and the others are authentic and vital literary versions of the real porch-sitters of Eatonville.

The language of *Their Eyes Were Watching God* radiates with the energy and the rhythm of Southern black speech. This talk might sound odd to white ears or black intellectuals. To Hurston, though, the proud, self-governing people of Eatonville were worthy speakers.

The noted African-American scholar Henry Louis Gates, Jr., has described *Their Eyes Were Watching God* as a "speakerly text."[5] By this he means the novel benefits greatly from being read aloud. The very sounds of the words give additional meaning to the text.

When Tea Cake describes to Janie a brawl in which he is involved, the strength of the phrasing and the figurative language itself makes the reader a witness to the fight. Hurston crafts Tea Cake's expression and dialect so carefully that he can be seen play-acting his speech:

Befo' he could bat his eye . . . Ah wuz all over

'im jus' lak gravy over rice. He lost his razor

tryin' tuh git loose from me. He wuz hollerin'

for me tuh turn him loose, but baby, Ah turnt

him every way *but* loose.[6]

Similarly, when Janie confides to Pheoby that "Ah'd sit dere wid de walls creepin' up on me and squeezin' all de life outa me,"[7] the reader feels suffocated along with her.

From the first page of *Their Eyes Were Watching God,* Hurston makes clear how much she values the telling of a good story:

It was the time to hear things and talk. These

sitters had been tongueless, earless, eyeless,

conveniences all day long. Mules and other

brutes had occupied their skins. But now the

sun and the bossman were gone, so the skins

felt powerful and human.[8]

At its center, *Their Eyes Were Watching God* is a novel about how common people talk and how they live.

CHAPTER 7

Reviews

In 1937, J. B. Lippincott published *Their Eyes Were
Watching God.* While the book would prove to be
Hurston's most popular novel, the first reviews
were mixed. White reviewers generally praised it,
and black reviewers were less complimentary.

To understand why reviewers were split along
racial lines is to understand the tenor of the
times. What is now called the Harlem Renaissance
was a period in the 1920s when African-American
writers and artists broke new ground with works
that celebrated their culture.

A term used alternatively with Harlem Renaissance was the "New Negro Movement." Conceived at that time by Howard University professor Alain Locke, the New Negro was an African American who created art—such as jazz, poetry, painting, or literature—while at the same time aspiring to bolster the image of the race.

In 1925, when Locke first coined his phrase, Harlem was a flourishing section of northern Manhattan, in New York City. More than one hundred thousand African Americans lived there, many of them recent migrants who had arrived from the South seeking work and a life free from the fear of lynch mobs.

Harlem resembled Eatonville, Florida, in many respects. African Americans owned businesses and served as doctors, firefighters, ministers, and musicians. To many blacks, Harlem was a haven from an unfriendly and often violent white world. As the poet Langston Hughes wrote at the time, "I was in love with Harlem long before I got there."[1]

The artists connected with the Harlem Renaissance were not the first noteworthy African-American writers, painters, and musicians, but they were among the first to call attention proudly to their race.

Hurston belonged to this artistic community and considered some of its best-known figures—poets Langston Hughes and Countee Cullen, and novelist Wallace Thurman—among her closest friends. Hurston enjoyed the famously lively Harlem nightlife as well. An acquaintance of hers said once, "When Zora was there, she *was* the party."[2]

Without question, Hurston helped shape this important cultural and literary movement. Yet she cannot be defined solely as a Harlem Renaissance writer. While she began writing in the 1920s, she did her best work, *Their Eyes Were Watching God,* in the 1930s.

Another important reason Hurston differed from some of the other Harlem Renaissance writers has more to do with her unique perspective. She first articulated this while at Barnard, in an essay she called "How It Feels to Be Colored Me":

> But I am not tragically colored. There is no great sorrow damned up in my soul, nor lurking behind my eyes. I do not mind at all. I do not belong to the sobbing school of Negrohood who hold that nature somehow has given them a lowdown dirty deal and whose feelings are all hurt about it. Even in the helter-skelter skirmish that is my life, I have seen that the world is to the strong regardless of a little pigmentation more or less. No, I do not weep at the world—I am too busy sharpening my oyster knife.[3]

Hurston's essay affirms a strong personal and unapologetic racial pride. She was never oblivious to racism and bore the brunt of its ugliness many times in her life. Yet, because Hurston saw blacks as having lives as full and complex as whites, in her writing she chose to celebrate the differences between the races rather than hide them.

Many of the leading African-American thinkers of the day objected to this viewpoint. To their minds, the mission of the New Negro was to promote their race and their art with equal gusto. This fundamental disagreement often made its way into the Harlem Renaissance writers' comments on Hurston's books.

In his review of *Their Eyes Were Watching God* for *Opportunity: A Journal of Negro Life,* then one of the most important African-American publications, Alain Locke voiced disapproval. In fewer than two hundred words, he took Hurston to task. While he conceded that her work was "folklore fiction at its best," he asked rhetorically, "when will the Negro novelist of maturity, who knows how to tell a story convincingly—which is Miss Hurston's cradle gift, come to grips with motive fiction and social document fiction?"[4]

Hurston was incensed by this critique. Not only did she believe passionately in the merits of folklore, she was particularly furious with Locke for presuming to tell her what kind of literature she should write. In a spirited rebuttal that the editors of *Opportunity* refused to publish, she claimed, "I will send my toenails to debate him on what he knows about Negroes and Negro life, and I will come personally to debate him on what he knows about literature on the subject."[5]

In the magazine *New Masses,* Richard Wright, who would later become known for his books *Black Boy* and *Native Son,* dismissed *Their Eyes Were Watching God* outright: "Miss Hurston seems to have no desire whatever to move in the direction of serious fiction."[6] To Wright, serious fiction meant literature that protests racism.

Wright went so far as to compare the characters in the novel to actors in a minstrel show, the infamous musicals in which whites performed in blackface and lampooned slavery: "Miss Hurston *voluntarily* continues in her novel the tradition which was *forced* upon the Negro in the theater, that is the minstrel technique that makes the 'white folks' laugh. Her characters eat and laugh and cry and work and kill; they swing like a pendulum eternally in that safe and narrow orbit in which America likes to see the Negro live: between laughter and tears."[7]

It was Hurston's use of an idiomatic Southern dialect that caused Wright to make his analogy. While Wright believed that the dialect's unrefined sound belittles its speakers, Hurston thought just the opposite. To her, Tea Cake's figurative language was every bit as integral to her story as the narrator's standard English.

Not all the reviews by African Americans of *Their Eyes Were Watching God* were negative. The poet and academic Sterling Brown applauded Hurston's use of dialect: "Miss Hurston's forte is the recording and the creation of folk-speech. Her devotion to these people has rewarded her; *Their Eyes Were Watching God* is chock-full of earthy and touching poetry."[8]

As a poet, Brown recognized the intrinsic value of Hurston's carefully chosen rich dialogue. As a rank-and-file Harlem Renaissance writer, he also noted what he saw in the book as evidence of strained race relations: "Living in an all-colored town, these people escape the worst pressures of caste and class. There is little harshness, there is enough money and work to go around. The author does not dwell upon the 'people ugly from ignorance and broken from being poor' who swarm around the 'muck' for short-time jobs. But here is bitterness . . ."[9]

White reviewers were generally positive. The *New York Times Book Review*'s Lucille Tompkins called *Their Eyes Were Watching God* "beautiful . . . a good deal of it is written in dialect, but really it is about every one, or at least every one who isn't so civilized that he has lost the capacity for glory."[10]

The reporter for the *New York Herald Tribune Weekly Book Review* wrote of Hurston, "Here is an author who writes with her head as well as with her heart."[11] A columnist for the *New York Post* likened her to famed English author D. H. Lawrence.[12]

Hurston's enthusiastic reception from the reviewers in white-owned newspapers would remain at odds with her failure to win over the black intellectuals who wanted her to protest racism. But, Hurston did not write *Their Eyes Were Watching God* as a protest novel.

White oppression never figures much in *Their Eyes Were Watching God* because Hurston believed that black culture was a worthy enough subject on its own. The conflict between black and white people was not as compelling an issue for her. The folk community Hurston depicts in her novel was one she treasured and saw no need to defend. The issue remains a hotly-debated topic among critics to this day.

CHAPTER 8

Primary Themes in the Novel

The Pear Tree

"Oh to be a pear tree—*any* tree in bloom!"[1]

The image of a blossoming tree as a metaphor for life appears many times in *Their Eyes Were Watching God*. It is first introduced when Janie is just sixteen. Like most teenage girls, she is entranced by the idea of love. The pear tree becomes Janie's image of a perfect natural love.

Nanny scoffs at this notion of ideal love. In her experience, the African-American woman accepts a lowly station in life, dwelling at the bottom of the social totem pole. White men and women, followed by black men, hold the keys to power. In order to keep from becoming "de mule uh de world," the black woman must protect herself. To Nanny, love is a juvenile and dangerous distraction.

When Janie kisses a village boy, Johnny Taylor, her grandmother takes immediate action. She marries Janie off to Logan Killicks, a prosperous "prop" for Janie "tuh lean on all yo' bawn days, and big protection."[2]

But Janie wants more than protection. She tells Nanny, "Ah wants things sweet wid mah marriage lak when you sit under a pear tree and think."[3] Logan provides none of this. He is so old and ugly that he ends up "desecrating the pear tree" for Janie.[4]

Janie's youthful innocence ends with her marriage to Logan. "She knew now that marriage did not make love. Janie's first dream was dead, so she became a woman."[5] Yet, while Janie's idealism is crushed, her spirit is not. She rebels and runs off with Joe Starks.

Joe plans to become a "big voice" in the world. While he may not resemble the Prince Charming Janie sees in her dreams, he is a man of great ambition and drive. Interestingly, this is another marriage of which Nanny would have approved. Janie agrees to trade romance—"sun-up and pollen and blooming trees"—for a comfortable life.[6]

But the sweet-talking Joe tricks Janie into a stifling and unequal marriage. He tells her that she cannot even speak without his permission. This second marriage proves as devoid of love as Janie's first.

With Tea Cake, everything is different from the start. Janie's original image of perfect love is restored. The pear tree comes into full bloom. "She couldn't make him look just like any other man to her. He looked like the love thoughts of women. He could be a bee to a blossom—a pear tree blossom in the spring."[7]

After Tea Cake's death, Janie gives away all of her possessions, save for a packet of seeds that "reminded Janie of Tea Cake more than anything else."[8] She plans to plant the seeds, a symbol of the near-perfect organic union she shared with Tea Cake. Presumably, of course, the seeds will produce yet another blossoming tree.

When she returns home to tell her story, *"Janie saw her life like a great tree in leaf with the things suffered,* things enjoyed, things done, and undone. Dawn and doom was in the branches."[9] Janie's metaphor of love as a pear tree, first defined in her youth, still resonates for her.

Janie's Quest

Their Eyes Were Watching God follows Janie Crawford on a quest to find what it means to be a strong and knowing person. Having been taught as a girl to "take a stand on high ground"[10] and "dream of what a woman oughta be and to do,"[11] Janie achieves these aims as an adult.

Though she runs away from the husband Nanny picks for her, Janie realizes early on in her second marriage that her circumstances have not changed for the better. Joe Starks no more values her as an individual than did Logan Killicks.

Like Logan, Joe wants property and prestige and a wife to help him with both. But, in fact, life with Joe is worse for Janie. He is an abusive, dominating presence. He views Janie only in terms of his own stature. He calls her "Mrs. Mayor Starks" and "pretty doll-baby." He forces her to hide her hair under a scarf. He believes her incapable of decision-making: "Somebody got to think for women and chillun and chickens and cows."[12] He refuses to let her talk in public, cutting her off when she is asked to make a speech.

Janie abides by Joe's will until the first time he hits her. From this point on, though outwardly complying, inside she rebels:

> Janie stood where he left her for unmeasured
> time and thought. She stood there until some-
> thing fell off the shelf inside her. Then she
> went inside there to see what it was. It was her

image of Jodie tumbled down and shattered.
But looking at it she saw that it never was the
flesh and blood figure of her dreams. Just
something she had grabbed up to drape her
dreams over . . . She was saving up feelings
for some man she had never seen. She had an
inside and an outside now and suddenly she
knew how not to mix them.[13]

With Logan, Janie sees no options for herself
other than to run away. With Joe, Janie begins to
understand herself more fully. She endures this difficult marriage by allowing herself to have a different
"inside and an outside" life. Janie hides her desires
but they wait, ready to erupt, just under the surface.

When Joe rudely ridicules her in the general
store, Janie fights back with her own stinging
words. Janie needs to attack Joe in order to begin
regaining control of her life. She belittles her
husband's masculinity, an insult from which he
does not recover. It can be said that Joe dies twice:
once when Janie kills him figuratively with her

words, and then again, just a few weeks later, when kidney disease overtakes him.

The Horizon

A recurring metaphor in the novel is the idea of the horizon. The horizon symbolizes Janie's quest for independence and self-acceptance. Literary critic Mary Helen Washington writes, "The horizon represents the outside world—the world of adventure where Janie journeyed in search of people and a value system that would allow her real self to shine."[14]

Joe Starks first appeals to Janie because "he spoke for far horizon. He spoke for change and chance."[15] When Joe proves instead to be a possessive tyrant, Janie realizes he will never be the man for her:

> She had been getting ready for her great journey to the horizons in search of *people;* it was important to all the world that she should find them and they find her. But she had been whipped like a cur dog, and run down the road after *things*.[16]

After Joe's death, Janie enjoys a new freedom and a growing self-confidence. When Tea Cake enters her life, she is ready for this loving relationship between equal partners. To Janie, Tea Cake is the "son of Evening Sun,"[17] an allusion to the horizon at its most vibrant time of day. Though Tea Cake cannot provide Janie with material comforts, he does something far better. He invites her to share in his adventures. Most important, he confirms her right to be herself.

At the very end of the book, Janie tells Pheoby, "Ah done been tuh de horizon and back and now ah kin set heah in mah house and live by comparisons."[18] While Janie is saddened by her circumstances, they have strengthened her: "She pulled in her horizon like a great fish-net. Pulled it from the waist of the world and draped it over her shoulder."[19] Though she has lost the love of her life, Janie Crawford's quest is a triumphant one. She has claimed her destiny and learned to celebrate herself as a person.

CHAPTER 9

Secondary Themes in the Novel

The Mule

More than a dozen pages of *Their Eyes Were Watching God* are concerned with the story of a mule. A commonly accepted metaphor for slavery, mules, like slaves, are bought and sold. More important, mules carry life's burdens with a stubborn strength.

The metaphor of the mule is obviously one that Hurston likes. She uses a mule in the name of her play *Mule Bone,* and again in the title of her folklore anthology, *Mules and Men.* In *Their Eyes Were Watching God.* the mule serves both as a stand-in for slavery, as well as a means to connect the novel to the animal tales central to African-American folklore.

At the novel's beginning, the narrator uses the image of the mule to contrast the peaceful Eatonville dusk with the difficult, workaday life of the typical resident: "These sitters had been tongueless, earless, eyeless conveniences all day long. Mules and other brutes occupied their skins. But now, the sun and the bossman were gone, so the skins felt powerful and human."[1]

In Janie's youth, Nanny describes to her a woeful version of the facts of life: men enjoy the power in society and a "woman is de mule uh de world."[2] Meaning to save her granddaughter from this fate as a beast of burden, Nanny arranges the marriage with old man Logan Killicks.

After many unhappy months it becomes clear that, despite Nanny's best intentions, Janie will not escape the metaphor of the mule unless she also escapes the marriage. In fact, in an ironic twist, Logan tries to patch things up with Janie by buying her a second mule, one that would be "all gentled up so even uh woman kin handle 'im."[3]

During Janie's marriage to Joe Starks, the mule resurfaces as a symbol. Matt Bonner, a man in town, owns a yellow mule that serves as a constant source of humor and conversation for the Eatonville porch-sitters. The animal is described in human terms: it looks like the Reverend, it drinks coffee, and it sleeps inside a neighbor's kitchen.

Merely to amuse themselves one afternoon, the porch-sitters mistreat the mule. When Janie voices her unhappiness with this, Joe buys the mule for a tiny amount of money. Like a slave, the mule's freedom is purchased.

At first glance, Starks's act seems charitable. A closer look reveals other motives. Ever the pompous "big-voice," Joe's desire to impress his constituents is more important to him than pleasing his wife. The five dollars he pays for the yellow mule's freedom is not that meaningful a sum for him, but astounds his neighbors.

Secondly, Joe's treatment of the mule is similar to his treatment of his wife. He provides materially for her but expects her compliance in return. Janie is Joe's possession every bit as much as the mule is. Her concern about the animal's tortured existence—"people ought to have some regard for helpless things"[4]—echoes feelings she has about her own life.

When the yellow mule dies, the town prepares to bury it in an elaborate mock funeral. Though she wants to attend the ceremony, Joe tells Janie it is improper for the mayor's wife, "goin' off in all dat mess uh commonness."[5] On the other hand, Joe uses the funeral to boost his own popularity. The speech he gives memorializing the poor creature "made him more solid than building the schoolhouse had done."[6]

The yellow mule and its funeral symbolize Janie Crawford's struggle with Joe Starks. As the "town escorted the carcass off . . . and left Janie standing in the doorway,"[7] the reader begins to suspect that Janie will not wait much longer to assert herself.

The Trial

After Janie kills Tea Cake, she must prove to a jury that she was acting in self-defense. The trial scene is the only one in the novel where whites are notably present and blacks are conspicuously powerless.

The trial is a disturbing and surreal episode, much like a bad dream. Janie is hustled into a courtroom a mere three hours following Tea Cake's death. Presumably, she is still in some sort of shock. The love of her life is dead by her own hands.

That Janie "must be tried that same day"[8] adds weight to the feeling of a dream sequence. In the real world, such a speedy rush to trial is a completely unlikely proposition. If anything, a poor African-American woman would be forced to languish in a jail cell before getting a trial.

Indeed, as an African-American woman in a Southern courtroom in the 1930s, Janie does not appear to stand a chance. Every one of the court's authority figures are white men: the police, the twelve members of the jury, the judge, the witnesses, and the lawyers.

A group of well-dressed white women with "the pinky color that comes of good food"[9] fill the public benches, adding to Janie's general unease. Interestingly, however, the fact that they are female diminishes the "us versus them" status in Janie's eyes. Privately, she wishes, in fact, that the women were her jury "instead of those menfolks."[10]

Even those who would seem to be on Janie's side are not. Tea Cake's friends are angry and confused over the circumstances surrounding his death. They are a hostile presence in the courtroom. The African-American community "were all against her, she could see. So many were there that a light slap from each one of them would have beat her to death. She felt them pelting her with dirty thoughts. They were there with their tongues cocked and loaded."[11]

For an extended period Janie remains silent, having little choice but to let the men in charge presume to tell the courtroom her story. These strangers "didn't know a thing about people like Tea Cake and her" but possess the power to "pass on what happened" and determine "whether things were done right or not."[12]

In a final effort to avenge his friend's death, Sop-de-Bottom interrupts the proceedings until he is warned that his own freedom is at risk. "If you know what's good for you, you better shut your mouth up until somebody calls you,"[13] the lawyer tells him condescendingly. While Janie's welfare appears to hold some sway in the court-room, the white men clearly have no interest in the sentiments of the black male community.

After Janie testifies on her own behalf, the trial ends. She awaits the jury's verdict, but with a twist: "It was not death she feared. It was misunderstanding. If they made a verdict that she didn't want Tea Cake and wanted him dead, then that was a real sin and a shame."[14]

In five minutes, however, Janie is acquitted of murder. In response, "the white women cried and stood around her like a protecting wall."[15] Despite the differences of race and social class, they relate to Janie's testimony as a universal love story.

Tea Cake's friends are not pleased by the verdict. The fact that they were silenced in the courtroom, on top of the finding of Janie's innocence, leads them to the angry conclusion that white men and black women are given preferential treatment over black men.

Race

The place in central Florida that Hurston always considered her real home was most unusual. Eatonville's natural advantages were abundant. In her autobiography, Hurston describes the "orange, grapefruit, tangerine, guavas and other fruits in our yard . . . a five acre garden with things to eat growing in it, and so we were never hungry."[16]

Yet the different community that was Eatonville resulted mainly from a charter written just four years before Hurston was born. This contract incorporated Eatonville, Florida, as a self-governing, all-African-American town.

Growing up in Eatonville, Hurston was shielded from the oppressive circumstances that defined the lives of the vast majority of Southern African Americans until the late 1960s. Beyond the sanctuary that was Eatonville, extreme poverty, political disenfranchisement, Jim Crow segregation, and brutal mob violence forced African Americans to wage a daily struggle for survival.

That Hurston came of age in a place where she not only felt safe but exalted as a black person informs much of her fiction. Critic Mary Helen Washington describes Eatonville and its influence on Hurston this way:

It was neither ghetto, nor slum, nor black bottom, but a rich source of black cultural traditions where Zora would be nourished on black folktales and tropical fruits and sheltered from the early contacts with racial prejudice that have so indelibly marked almost all other Afro-American writers.[17]

In *Their Eyes Were Watching God,* black characters loom large amid a smattering of white characters. As another critic explains:

Hurston's social protest comes in the form of decentering the white presence in her celebration of the fullness of black existence, a fullness maintained and sustained despite the oppressive political, social, and historical status of black people. White people in the novel are present, but only marginally. Hence, Hurston's colorful characters emerge gracefully and skillfully to take center stage in this black cultural extravaganza.[18]

Hurston neither condones nor is oblivious to racism. But because she does not view her race as an impediment—it is never, as she puts it, "a low-down dirty deal"[19]—she is less interested in protesting black–white relationships than she is in investigating them.

Hurston's inquiry begins at the novel's outset with a description of the Eatonville residents unwinding on their porches after a long day on the job for the white "bossman." At work "these sitters had been tongueless, earless, eyeless conveniences."[20] It is only after they return home that they are able to reclaim their identities, becoming "lords of sounds and lesser things."[21]

Hurston examines the legacy of slavery through the character of Nanny. Slave memories serve to shape her view of the world as a degrading place for the African-American woman. Nanny laments, "Ah didn't want to be used for a work-ox and a brood sow . . . It sho wasn't mah will for things to happen lak they did."[22] Nanny's experiences lead her to advise Janie to seek material security over love. The African-American woman is powerless, Nanny believes, so she better figure out how others will take care of her.

Through Joe Starks, Hurston illustrates the concept of striving to achieve economic and social equality. One of Joe's most obvious failings is his desire to mimic the habits of the white middle class. When Janie first meets Joe, he reminds her of Mr. Washburn, the white man for whom her grandmother worked. Joe buys a big white house in Eatonville that makes the other homes in town look like "servants' quarters surrounding the 'big house.'"[23] Joe is a loud-mouthed buffoon whom Hurston uses to poke fun at the idea of a black man who thinks he will achieve more if he "acts white."

Through Mrs. Turner, Hurston comments on the African-American community's own deep-seated prejudices. Mrs. Turner "sought out Janie to friend with" because she admired her "coffee-and-cream complexion and her luxurious hair."[24] To this racist woman, light-skinned African Americans are superior to those with darker coloring. She tells Janie, "It's too many black folks already. We oughta lighten up de race."[25] As she does with Joe, Hurston (in the voice of her narrator) mocks Mrs. Turner's intolerance:

> Behind her crude words was a belief that somehow she and others through worship could attain her paradise—a heaven of straight-haired, thin-lipped, high-nose boned white seraphs. The physical impossibilities in no way injured faith.[26]

The hurricane and its aftermath underscore racial tensions in a more straightforward manner than in other parts of the novel. Janie is cautioned about the storm's coming by Native American Seminoles who recognize nature's warning signs. But instead of heading to higher ground, Janie ignores their warnings, muttering to herself, "Indians are dumb anyhow, always were."[27]

Following the storm, armed white guards force Tea Cake to help bury the dead. In the Jim Crow South, even corpses are not treated equally. Tea Cake is told that white bodies will be put in coffins and the others in a mass grave.

During Janie's trial, the same Jim Crow laws prohibit African Americans from serving on juries. Janie's life hangs in the balance while an all-white jury and white judge determine whether she will be executed for Tea Cake's murder. Though Janie does speak on her own behalf, ultimately, it is the testimony of the white doctor who attends to Tea Cake that appears to sway the jury.

The African Americans present in the courtroom are forced to stand in the back, "packed tight like a case of celery."[28] Despite the fact that speech is often "the only real weapon left to weak folks,"[29] the blacks are ignored or silenced outright by the whites. The courtroom scene painfully details the sanctioned segregation that treated African Americans as second-class citizens.

CHAPTER 10

Zora Neale Hurston's Other Books

Jonah's Gourd Vine (1934)

This novel has its roots in a short story Zora Neale Hurston published a year before in the literary magazine *Story*. Entitled "The Gilded Six-Bits," it tells a tale of love and conflict between Missie May and Joe, a young couple from Eatonville, Florida. The president of J. B. Lippincott, one of the most important publishing companies in the country, read the story and was so impressed by it he asked Hurston if she had a novel he might publish.

Hurston had been considering writing something longer for a while, but as she described in her autobiography, "the idea of attempting a book seemed so big, that I gazed at it in the quiet of the night, but hid it away from even myself in daylight."[1]

Still, Hurston realized the potential value of Lippincott's offer and went to work immediately. She was nearly penniless at this time. She rented a one-room house for $1.50 a week and managed to survive on a mere fifty cents a week for groceries her cousin lent her. She borrowed the two dollars she needed to mail the manuscript to the publisher in New York.

Less than a month later, Hurston received a telegram with a two-hundred-dollar advance and the welcome news that her book would be published. Of this event she wrote later, "I never expect to have a greater thrill than that wire gave me."[2]

Jonah's Gourd Vine is in many regards a fictionalized account of the Hurston family. Its main characters are named John and Lucy, after Hurston's own parents. The book's dialogue and folk stories draw directly from Hurston's youth in the rural South.

The novel follows John's character most closely. The son of a slave, John teaches himself to read and becomes a minister. John has great physical strength and a charismatic personality, but he is unfaithful to his wife and his congregation turns him out.

Lucy becomes sick and battles courageously against her illness. On her deathbed, John loses his temper and hits her. The book's title comes from the Bible (Jonah 4: 6-10) and refers to this act of violence. In a letter to a friend, Hurston explains, "You see the prophet of God sat up under a gourd vine that had grown up in one night. But a cut worm came along and cut it down. Great and sudden growth. One act of malice and it is withered and gone."[3]

Book reviewers liked *Jonah's Gourd Vine* so much that it was selected for the national Book-of-the-Month Club. J. B. Lippincott liked it so much it agreed to publish Hurston's collection of folklore the following year.

Mules and Men (1935)

I'm like that old mule—

Black—and don't give a damn!

You got to take me

Like I am.

—Langston Hughes, "Me and the Mule"[4]

Hurston entitled her folklore anthology *Mules and Men* to draw attention to the connections between a mule's situation and a slave's. Like slaves, mules are sold on an open market and forced to work under harsh conditions. Even more important as a metaphor for a slave society, mules are tough and stubborn and able to survive under duress.

The 1936 book jacket for *Mules and Men*.

Hurston began collecting folklore in 1927 as a student of Franz Boas, the most important American anthropology scholar of the era. After four years of collecting oral history throughout the Deep South, Hurston wrote the anthology that dominates the field to this day.

Literary critic and scholar Arnold Rampersad praises Hurston and *Mules and Men*: "Here she came to terms at last with the full range of black folk traditions, practices, expressions, and types of behavior, and began to trust her understanding of their multiple meanings as an index to the African-American world."[5]

The anthology includes seventy folk stories, five descriptions of encounters with voodoo doctors, and an annotated appendix. Rampersad notes the influence of this folklore on Hurston's fiction, most notably in the case of *Their Eyes Were Watching God*.[6]

Tell My Horse (1938)

For a number of months in 1936 and 1937, Hurston lived in the Caribbean researching voodoo. Voodoo—or hoodoo, or conjure, as it is often called—is a traditional set of religious practices. At its core is the belief that the voodoo doctor can harness spirits to change circumstances.

Hurston's living expenses in the West Indies were paid through grants made to her by the prestigious Guggenheim Foundation. In remote areas of Jamaica, and then Haiti, Hurston witnessed many extreme and intense practices, including animal sacrifices and séances.

In an isolated part of the jungle in Haiti, Hurston was likely poisoned by an unfriendly conjurer. "For a whole day and night," she wrote the president of the Guggenheim Foundation, "I'd thought I'd never make it."[7]

As soon as she recovered enough to travel, Hurston returned to Florida to write *Tell My Horse,* a combination travel and voodoo guide to Haiti. Perhaps its most sensational section deals with zombies. A zombie is a corpse that appears to have come back to life. In her autobiography, Hurston writes that her "greatest thrill was coming face to face with a zombie and photographing her."[8]

Tell My Horse met with mixed reviews, but a columnist for the *New York Herald Tribune* was so impressed he suggested Hurston write five more books on voodoo.[9]

Moses, Man of the Mountain (1939)

Moses, Man of the Mountain is quite different from Hurston's other books. It is her longest novel, a retelling of the biblical story of Moses that draws parallels between the enslaved Israelites and Africans.

In the fashion of a long fable, Hurston transforms the traditional biblical figure of Moses into an all-powerful black voodoo doctor. He marries the "warm brown" Zipporah and studies magic from his friend Jethro, for whom "other people's thoughts are like glass."[10] Moses begins speaking in the dialect of rural African Americans, often to purposefully comic results.

Yet while much of *Moses, Man of the Mountain* is meant to be humorous, its central message—that of the essential importance of freedom—is a solemn one. Just as the Jews struggled to emancipate themselves from Pharoah, so do the slaves in the African-American tradition.

Dust Tracks on a Road (1942)

At the request of her publisher, Zora Neale Hurston reluctantly wrote her autobiography when she was fifty-one years old. While the first portion of the book reads like a traditional autobiography and is especially useful for understanding her relationship with her parents, much of the rest does not. As Hurston confesses, "I did not want to write it at all, because it is too hard to reveal one's inner self."[11]

It is certain that Hurston made up significant parts of the book. Scholar Henry Louis Gates, Jr., compares her to "a masquerader putting on a disguise for the ball, like a character in her fictions."[12] Biographer Robert Hemenway writes that *Dust Tracks on a Road* "reaffirm(s) the vital source of her fiction."[13] In fact, Hemenway continues, "That is the chief value of her autobiography—its documentation of the Eatonville scene and what it meant to a woman who would rise by force of will and talent to become nationally known."[14] Author Alice Walker, for whom Hurston is a literary deity, bluntly disparages her work in this single instance: "For me, the most unfortunate thing Zora ever wrote is her autobiography. After the first several chapters, it rings false."[15]

Yet while much of *Dust Tracks on a Road* wanders off the point of Hurston's life, the book is still a wonderfully engaging read. Its greatest merit lies in its examination and use of distinct dialect and character—the essential elements of her best fiction. It is worth noting as well the book was Hurston's most commercially successful for many years.

Seraph on the Suwanee (1948)

Seraph on the Suwanee is the story of the troubled marriage of a white couple, Jim and Arvay

Merserve. Though Hurston once compared Arvay's doomed search for selfhood to Janie Crawford's, it is a hollow comparison. The novel fails in many ways.

To understand how Hurston might have written such an inferior book, it may be useful to note an observation of Henry Louis Gates, Jr.: "Put simply, Hurston wrote well when she was comfortable, wrote poorly when she was not."[16]

The late 1940s were the beginning of a devastatingly difficult decade for Hurston. Financial and personal problems were huge and unceasing. Her writing in *Seraph on the Suwanee* may have suffered as a result of the economic and psychological pressures she was facing. Indeed, as Robert Hemenway remarks, "The book itself is not nearly so interesting as the authorial emotions that coalesced in the creating of it."[17]

CHAPTER 11

Legacy

The author and political activist June Jordan describes *Their Eyes Were Watching God* as the "most successful, convincing and exemplary novel of blacklove that we have. Period."[1] Jordan is referring, specifically, to Janie and Tea Cake's mutually devoted relationship.

Yet, as one of Zora Neale Hurston's biographers, Valerie Boyd, points out, "Hurston's novel is ultimately about self-love, about Janie's hard-willed choice to love nobody—not even the love of her life—more than she does herself."[2]

For much of *Their Eyes Were Watching God,* Janie searches for self through her relationships with men. Because Nanny has steered her in the wrong direction, encouraging her to marry for security, Janie cannot conceive of a different life. Neither Logan Killicks nor Joe Starks permits her to be her own person and speak her own mind. For a long time, Janie does not even realize she has the ability to do so.

Tea Cake treats Janie as his equal from the beginning, but it is only when Janie accepts herself in this way that she becomes a truly independent woman. Janie comes to understand that she is the equal of any man and that her thoughts and words are as important. It is Janie—and Janie alone—who "pulled in her horizon like a great fish-net."

Because Janie eventually claims her right to self-hood, many critics have touted *Their Eyes Were Watching God* as a feminist novel. What has proven more controversial among critics is whether or not the novel qualifies as African-American "protest literature."

For the author Richard Wright, the answer is an unequivocal no. Wright believed that Hurston's use of an authentic Southern African-American dialect actually encourages racism. He scoffed at what he saw as the novel's exclusive focus on the optimistic aspects of African-American life, while ignoring its painful difficulties.

But for Hurston, affirming African-American culture is precisely the point. She makes no apologies for drawing on the community of her youth in *Their Eyes Were Watching God*. Hurston's Eatonville roots provide her with a healthy confidence in her race. Despite the unfortunate truth that few African Americans, particularly those in the South, are able to share the kind of experience she enjoys growing up there, Hurston never chooses to hide its advantages.

From a very young age, she understands that black lives are every bit as rich and interesting as white lives. What is more, she is more concerned with investigating how blacks live together than how they live among whites.

As Valerie Boyd comments, "In this way, *Their Eyes Were Watching God* becomes protest literature on yet another level: It protests white oppression by stripping it of its potency, by denying its all-powerfulness in black people's lives."[3] Indeed, with the exception of the trial scene, white people make few appearances in the novel.

In actuality, however, Hurston never means to protest as much as she means to celebrate. It is not the conflict between the races that motivates her writing. What moves Hurston is African-American culture—the good and the bad—entirely on its own.

Alice Walker has written at length about the considerable influence Hurston has had on her, as a writer and a woman. (Stuck on a desert island, Walker says she would have *Mules and Men* and *Their Eyes Were Watching God* with her.)[4] What she sees as "most characteristic of Zora's work [is] racial health; a sense of black people as complete, complex, *undiminished* human beings."[5]

In a direct reproach to Richard Wright, Walker applauds Hurston's use of regional dialect: "She took the trouble to capture the beauty of rural black expression. She saw poetry where other writers merely saw failure to cope with English. She was so at ease with her blackness it never occurred to her that she should act one way among blacks and another among whites (as her more 'sophisticated' black critics apparently did)."[6]

After many careful readings of *Their Eyes Were Watching God,* Walker composed a poem about Janie Crawford. The poem declared that "A woman, unless she submits,/ is neither a mule/ nor a queen."[7] To

Zora sought to capture the beauty of her community in her work. Here she is with three boys in Eatonville, 1935.

Walker, Janie is a model woman, "a heroine . . . indispensable to my own growth, my own life."[8]

Walker has said much the same about Janie's creator. She describes Hurston as "a writer of courage, and incredible humor, with poetry in every line."[9] Indeed, Walker's unending support of Hurston, combined with Robert Hemenway's 1977 definitive biography, brought the author back into the public eye.

When Hurston died in January 1960, not a single one of her books was still in print. She died broke, alone, and unknown. In 1972, Walker would make her now-famous pilgrimage to Florida seeking Hurston's grave and publish her essay entitled "Looking For Zora."

The University of Illinois Press published the Hemenway biography and, based on the author's recommendation, bought the rights to *Their Eyes Were Watching God* for a pittance from J. B. Lippincott, the original publisher. It is now published in paperback by HarperCollins to enormous commercial success.

As profitable as the book has proven to be, its critical achievement is even greater. Censured by prominent African-American writers when it was first published in 1937, for Hurston's perceived failure to champion her race, the novel lay condemned for the next four decades. Literary scholar Michael Awkward has observed, "Afro-American intellectuals were involved in a battle over whether to emphasize likeness or difference, Americanness or blackness. This was a battle which, coupled with the added burden of her gender that rendered Hurston marginal to begin with, made full appreciation of her talents virtually impossible during the first half of the twentieth century."[10]

Seventy years later, *Their Eyes Were Watching God* is commonly described as a "classic" novel. It is taught in schools around the country and dissected by scholars and critics. Henry Louis Gates, Jr., has written, "Hurston is the first writer that [his] generation of black and feminist critics has brought into the canon . . . [She] is now a cardinal figure in the Afro-American canon, the feminist canon, and the canon of American fiction."[11]

In her autobiography, *Dust Tracks on a Road,* Hurston provides intimate details of the relationship in her life that serves as the model for Janie and Tea Cake. In 1935, when she was forty-four, Hurston became involved with a twenty-three-year-old Columbia University graduate student named Percival McGuire Punter.

As she put it most colorfully, "I did not just fall in love. I made a parachute jump."[12] Like most students, Punter had no money, but in Hurston's eyes "had what it takes—a bright soul, a fine mind in a fine body, and courage."[13] For the first time in her life, Hurston was thoroughly smitten: "He was so extraordinary that I lived in terrible fear lest women camp on his doorstep in droves and take him away from me."[14]

Yet, when Punter asked her to marry him and forgo her career, Hurston cut the relationship short. "I had things clawing inside of me that must be said," she explained simply.[15] Fleeing to Haiti on a research fellowship, those "clawing things" became the novel *Their Eyes Were Watching God*.

Though Hurston would write later, "I tried to embalm all the tenderness of my passion for him,"[16] the book's love affair is inspired by, but does not attempt to replicate, the real-life affair. While general similarities exist, the traveling gambler, Tea Cake Woods, is not the college man, Percival Punter.

More to the point, Janie Crawford is not Zora Neale Hurston. Both are nonconformists willing to go out on a limb for what they believe. But Janie searches for herself through her relationships with men, eventually acquiring the strength and wisdom to claim her identity. Hurston's selfhood is intact all along. Hurston ends her love affair with Punter when he demands "that one thing I could not do"—that is, to stop writing.[17]

As is the case with all her fiction, Hurston draws from personal experience in *Their Eyes Were*

Watching God. The story is based on her life most obviously in that it deals with the relationship of an older woman and a younger man. Yet, despite its personal aspects, the novel is much more than a simple torrent of emotions.

What Richard Wright and Alain Locke found most troubling about the book is, in fact, its greatest strength. The folklore traditions that Hurston pursued with the trained eye of the anthropologist engage the reader and play a vital role in preserving the cultural heritage of African Americans.

Their Eyes Were Watching God broke new ground celebrating folk traditions, particularly of African-American women. The black intellectuals' claim that Hurston was disloyal to her people by sharing their rituals with white readers rings false. The jokes, stories, and dialects that Hurston presented in the book never betray the African-American tradition, but rather honor it.

CHRONOLOGY

1891   Zora Neale Hurston is born in Notasulga, Alabama, on January 7.

1892   The Hurston family moves to Eatonville, Florida.

1904   Zora's mother, Lucy Potts Hurston, dies.

1905   Zora's father, John Hurston, remarries; Zora is sent to boarding school in Jacksonville, Florida.

1919   Enters college at Howard University in Washington, D.C.

1925   Wins first writing prize. Transfers to Barnard College in New York City on full scholarship.

1926   Begins work with renowned anthropologist Franz Boas.

1927   Marries Herbert Sheen.

1929   Takes part in folklore and voodoo research expeditions.

1931   Divorces Sheen.

1933   Writes and produces play entitled *The Great Day*; short story "The Gilded Six-Bits" attracts publisher J. B. Lippincott.

1934   *Jonah's Gourd Vine* is published.

1935   *Mules and Men* is published.

1936   Receives Guggenheim fellowship to travel and study in Jamaica and Haiti; writes *Their Eyes Were Watching God*.

1937   *Their Eyes Were Watching God* is published.

1938   *Tell My Horse* is published.

1939   *Moses, Man of the Mountain* is published. Marries Albert Price.

1942   Publishes autobiography, *Dust Tracks on a Road*.

1943   Purchases houseboat in Florida; divorces Price.

1944   Marries James Pitts.

1948 *Seraph on Sewanee* is published.

1960 Dies of a stroke on January 28.

1973 Author Alice Walker sponsors a headstone for Hurston's grave.

Chapter 1. On the Author

1. Alice Walker, *In Search of Our Mothers' Gardens* (Orlando, Fla.: Harcourt, Inc., 1983), p. 86.

2. Zora Neale Hurston, *Dust Tracks on a Road* (New York: HarperPerennial, 1996), p. 1.

3. Ibid., p. 70.

4. Ibid., p. 207.

5. Ibid., p. 208.

6. Walker, p. 107.

Chapter 2. Plot Summary and Analysis

1. Zora Neale Hurston, *Their Eyes Were Watching God* (New York: HarperCollins, 2000), p. 2.

2. Claire Crabtree, "The Confluence of Folklore, Feminism, and Black Self-Determination in Zora Neale Hurston's *Their Eyes Were Watching God*," in *Southern Literary Journal*, vol. 17, Spring 1985, pp. 54–66.

3. Henry Louis Gates, Jr., "*Their Eyes Were Watching God*: Hurston and the Speakerly Text," in *Zora Neale Hurston: Critical Perspectives Past and Present,* ed. Henry Louis Gates, Jr., and K. A. Appiah (New York: Amistad Press, 1993), p. 168.

4. Hurston, p. 20.

5. Ibid., p. 16.

6. Ibid., p. 14.

7. Ibid., p. 26.

8. Ibid., p. 27.

9. Ibid., p. 30.

10. Ibid., p. 55.

11. Ibid., p. 48.

12. Ibid., p. 55.

13. Ibid., p. 19.

14. Ibid., p. 118.

15. Ibid., p. 153.

Chapter 3. Character Study: Janie Crawford

1. Houston A. Baker, Jr., quoted in Nellie McKay, "'Crayon Enlargements of Life': Zora Neale Hurston's *Their Eyes Were Watching God* as Autobiography," in *New Essays* on *"Their Eyes Were Watching God,"* ed. Michael Awkward (New York: Cambridge University Press, 1990), p. 67.

2. Zora Neale Hurston, *Their Eyes Were Watching God* (New York: HarperCollins, 2000), p. 19.

3. Ibid., p. 15.

4. Ibid., p. 17.

5. Ibid.

6. Ibid., p. 51.

7. Ibid., p. 84.

8. Ibid., p. 85.

9. Ibid., p. 102.

10. Ibid., p. 151.

11. Ibid., p. 158.

12. Ibid., p. 173.

13. Mary Helen Washington, "I Love the Way Janie Crawford Left Her Husbands," in *"Their Eyes Were Watching God"*: A Casebook, ed. Cheryl A. Wall (New York: Oxford University Press, 2000), p. 33.

14. Hurston, p. 227.

15. Ibid.

Chapter 4. Character Studies: Janie Crawford's Men

1. Zora Neale Hurston, *Their Eyes Were Watching God* (New York: HarperCollins, 2000), p. 28.

2. Ibid., p. 29.

3. Ibid., p. 30

4. Ibid., p. 34.

5. Ibid., p. 35.

6. Ibid., p. 58.

7. Ibid.

8. Ibid., p. 34.

9. Ibid., p. 103.

10. Ibid., p. 119.

11. Ibid., p. 129.

12. Ibid., p. 158.

13. Ibid., p. 115.

14. Ibid., p. 114.

15. Ibid., p. 129.

16. Ibid., p. 147.

17. Ibid., p. 172.

Chapter 5. Character Studies: Minor Characters

1. Zora Neale Hurston, *Their Eyes Were Watching God* (New York: HarperCollins, 2000), p. 107.

2. Ibid., p. 19.

3. Ibid.

4. Ibid., p. 226.

5. Ibid., p. 155.

Chapter 6. Folklore and Language

1. Zora Neale Hurston, *Mules and Men* (New York: HarperPerennial, 1990), p. 1.

2. Zora Neale Hurston, *Dust Tracks on a Road* (New York: HarperPerennial, 1996), pp. 143–144.

3. Hurston, *Mules and Men*, p. 2.

4. Zora Neale Hurston, *Their Eyes Were Watching God* (New York: HarperCollins, 2000), p. 158.

5. Henry Louis Gates, Jr., "*Their Eyes Were Watching God*: Hurston and the Speakerly Text," in *Zora Neale Hurston: Critical Perspectives Past and Present,* ed. Henry Louis Gates, Jr., and K. A. Appiah (New York: Amistad Press, 1993), pp. 154–203.

6. Hurston, *Their Eyes Were Watching God,* p. 150.

7. Ibid., p. 133.

8. Ibid., pp. 1–2.

Chapter 7. Reviews

1. Steven Watson, *The Harlem Renaissance: Hub of African-American Culture, 1920–1930* (New York: Pantheon Books, 1995), p. 50.

2. Valerie Boyd, *Wrapped in Rainbows: The Life of Zora Neale Hurston* (New York: Scribner, 2003), p. 95.

3. Zora Neale Hurston, "How It Feels to Be Colored Me," American Studies at the University of Virginia, n.d., <http://xroads.virginia.edu/~MA01/Grand-Jean/Hurston/Chapters/how.html> (August 14, 2008).

4. Alain Locke, review of *Their Eyes Were Watching God, Opportunity: A Journal of Negro Life,* June 1, 1938, reprinted in *Zora Neale Hurston: Critical Perspectives Past and Present,* ed. Henry Louis Gates, Jr., and K. A. Appiah (New York: Amistad Press, 1993), p. 18.

5. Robert E. Hemenway, *Zora Neale Hurston: A Literary Biography* (Urbana, Ill.: University of Illinois Press, 1980), p. 242.

6. Richard Wright, untitled article, *New Masses,* October 5, 1937, reprinted in Gates and Appiah, p. 16.

7. Ibid., p.17.

8. Sterling Brown, "Luck is a Fortune," *Nation,* October 16, 1937, reprinted in Gates and Appiah, p. 20.

9. Ibid.

10. Lucille Tompkins, "In the Florida Glades," *New York Times Book Review*, September 26, 1937, reprinted in Gates and Appiah, p. 18.

11. Sheila Hibben, "Vibrant Book Full of Nature and Salt," *New York Herald Tribune Weekly Book Review*, September 26, 1937, reprinted in Gates and Appiah, p. 21.

12. Hemenway, p. 241.

Chapter 8. Primary Themes in the Novel

1. Zora Neale Hurston, *Their Eyes Were Watching God* (New York: HarperCollins, 2000), p. 14.

2. Ibid., p. 27.

3. Ibid., p. 29.

4. Ibid., p. 17.

5. Ibid., p. 30.

6. Ibid., p. 35.

7. Ibid., p. 126.

8. Ibid., p. 225.

9. Ibid., p. 10.

10. Ibid., p. 20.

11. Ibid., p. 19.

12. Ibid., p. 83.

13. Ibid., p. 85.

14. Mary Helen Washington, "I Love the Way Janie Crawford Left Her Husbands" in *"Their Eyes Were Watching God": A Casebook*, ed. Cheryl A. Wall (New York: Oxford University Press, 2000), p. 36.

15. Hurston, p. 35.

16. Ibid., p. 106.

17. Ibid., p. 209.

18. Ibid., p. 225.

19. Ibid., p. 227.

Chapter 9. Secondary Themes in the Novel

1. Zora Neale Hurston, *Their Eyes Were Watching God* (New York: HarperCollins, 2000), pp. 1–2.

2. Ibid., p. 17.

3. Ibid., p. 32.

4. Ibid., p. 67.

5. Ibid., p. 71.

6. Ibid.

7. Ibid.

8. Ibid., p. 217.

9. Ibid.

10. Ibid.

11. Ibid., p. 218.

12. Ibid., p. 217.

13. Ibid., p. 219.

14. Ibid., p. 221.

15. Ibid.

16. Zora Neale Hurston, *Dust Tracks on a Road* (New York: HarperPerennial, 1996), p. 12.

17. Mary Helen Washington, from the Introduction to *I Love Myself When I Am Laughing . . . and Then Again When I Am Looking Mean and Impressive: A Zora Neale Hurston Reader*, ed. Alice Walker (New York: The Feminist Press, 1979), p. 9.

18. Neal A. Lester, *Understanding Zora Neale Hurston's "Their Eyes Were Watching God": A Student Casebook to Issue, Sources, and Historical Documents* (Westport, Conn.: Greenwood Press, 1999), p. 90.

19. Zora Neale Hurston, "How It Feels to Be Colored Me," American Studies at the University of Virginia, n.d., <http://xroads.virginia.edu/~MA01/Grand-Jean/Hurston/Chapters/how.html> (August 14, 2008).

20. Hurston, *Their Eyes Were Watching God*, p. 1.

21. Ibid., p. 2.

22. Ibid., p. 19.

23. Ibid., pp. 55–56.

24. Ibid., p. 164.

25. Ibid., p. 165.

26. Ibid., p. 170.

27. Ibid., p. 181.

28. Ibid., p. 218.

29. Ibid.

Chapter 10. Zora Neale Hurston's Other Books

1. Zora Neale Hurston, *Dust Tracks on a Road* (New York: HarperPerennial, 1996), p. 171.

2. Ibid., p. 175.

3. Carla Kaplan, *Zora Neale Hurston: A Life in Letters* (New York: Doubleday, 2002), p. 291.

4. Langston Hughes, "Me and the Mule," Old Poetry, n.d., <http://oldpoetry.com/opoem/57389-Langston-Hughes-Me-And-The-Mule> (August 14, 2008).

5. Arnold Rampersad, Foreword to *Mules and Men* (New York: HarperPerennial, 1990), xvi–xvii.

6. Ibid.

7. Kaplan, p. 403.

8. Hurston, p. 168.

9. Valerie Boyd, *Wrapped in Rainbows: The Life of Zora Neale Hurston* (New York: Scribner, 2003), pp. 321–322.

10. Zora Neale Hurston, *Moses, Man of the Mountain* (New York: HarperPerennial, 1991), pp. 101–102.

11. Robert Hemenway, *Zora Neale Hurston: A Literary Biography* (Urbana, Ill.: University of Illinois Press, 1980), p. 278.

12. Henry Louis Gates, Jr., Afterword to *Dust Tracks*, p. 294.

13. Hemenway, p. 277.

14. Ibid.

15. Alice Walker, *In Search of Our Mothers' Gardens* (Orlando, Fla.: Harcourt, Inc., 1983), p. 91.

16. Gates, Afterword to *Dust Tracks,* p. 296.

17. Hemenway, p. 314.

Chapter 11. Legacy

1. June Jordan, "On Richard Wright and Zora Neale Hurston: Notes Toward a Balancing of Love and Hatred," *Black World,* August 1974, p. 5.

2. Valerie Boyd, *Wrapped In Rainbows: The Life of Zora Neale Hurston* (New York: Scribner, 2003), p. 304.

3. Ibid., p. 305.

4. Alice Walker, *In Search of Our Mothers' Gardens* (Orlando, Fla.: Harcourt, Inc., 1983), p. 86.

5. Ibid., p. 85.

6. Ibid., p. 261.

7. Ibid., p. 7.

8. Ibid.

9. Ibid., p. 260.

10. Michael Awkward, ed., *New Essays on "Their Eyes Were Watching God"* (New York: Cambridge University Press, 1990), p. 11.

11. Henry Louis Gates, Jr., *The Signifying Monkey: A Theory of Afro-American Literary Criticism* (New York: Oxford University Press, 1988), p. 180.

12. Zora Neale Hurston, *Dust Tracks on a Road* (New York: HarperPerennial, 1996), p. 205.

13. Ibid., p. 207.

14. Ibid.

15. Ibid., p. 208.

16. Ibid., p. 211.

17. Ibid., p. 208.

antithesis—The opposite of something; for example, the hideous monster was the antithesis of the beautiful princess.

bootlegger—A person who makes or sells liquor illegally.

canon—In literature, a comprehensive list of books within a specific field of study.

chauvinist—A person who believes in the superiority of his or her own kind.

confidant—A close friend or associate with whom secrets or private matters are shared; spelled confidante for a female.

flashback—A literary device in which an event that occurs before the present time in the story is inserted in the narrative.

idiomatic—Expressions in a particular language or dialect that are not predictable from the usual meanings of the words; for example, "he was just pulling your leg" is an idiomatic expression in English.

indigenous—Native, or original to, a particular region or country.

itinerant—A person who travels from place to place, usually working short-term laboring jobs.

Jim Crow laws—Public discrimination against, and segregation of, African Americans in the southern United States.

legacy—Something handed down or inherited from the past.

nonconformist—A person who refuses to follow established customs or attitudes.

omniscient—Having perfect knowledge and understanding of all things.

posthumously—Occurring after death.

stature—An achieved level of respect.

Books

1934   *Jonah's Gourd Vine*

1935   *Mules and Men*

1937   *Their Eyes Were Watching God*

1938   *Tell My Horse*

1939   *Moses, Man of the Mountain*

1942   *Dust Tracks on a Road*

1948   *Seraph on the Suwanee*

Short Stories

1921   "John Redding Goes to Sea"

1924   "Drenched in Light"

1925   "Spunk"

       "Under the Bridge"

       "Magnolia Flower"

1926   "Muttsy"

       "Sweat"

1933   "The Gilded Six-Bits"

1934   "The Fire and the Cloud"

1941   "Cock Robin, Beale Stret"

1942   "Story in Harlem Slang"

FURTHER READING

Books

Awkward, Michael, ed. *New Essays on "Their Eyes Were Watching God."* New York: Cambridge University Press, 1990.

Boyd, Valerie. *Wrapped in Rainbows: The Life of Zora Neale Hurston.* New York: Scribner, 2003.

Gates, Henry Louis, Jr., and K. A., Appiah, eds. *Zora Neale Hurston: Critical Perspectives Past and Present.* New York: Amistad Press, 1993.

Hemenway, Robert E. *Zora Neale Hurston: A Literary Biography.* Urbana, Ill.: University of Illinois Press, 1980.

Kaplan, Carla, ed. *Zora Neale Hurston: A Life in Letters.* New York: Doubleday, 2002.

Walker, Alice, ed. *I Love Myself When I Am Laughing . . . and Then Again When I Am Looking Mean and Impressive: A Zora Neale Hurston Reader.* New York: The Feminist Press at The City University of New York, 1979.

Wall, Cheryl, ed. *Zora Neale Hurston's "Their Eyes Were Watching God": A Casebook.* New York: Oxford University Press, 2000.

Internet Addresses

The Official Zora Neale Hurston Web site

http://zoranealehurston.com/

Online Classroom: Zora Neale Hurston

http://www.floridamemory.com/OnlineClassroom/zora_hurston/

Zora Neale Hurston Institute for Documentary Studies

http://www.zoranealehurston.ucf.edu/

INDEX

Nanny
  character study, 17, 39–40
  motivations, 18, 24, 25, 31, 40
  philosophy of life, 18–19, 28,
      67–68, 76, 85–86
  slavery as formative, 18, 24, 40

Oral traditions, 15, 16, 23, 42, 48,
    52–53

Porch-sitters, 41–42, 76, 77, 85
poverty, 6, 46, 90
Punter, Percival McGuire, 13, 14,
    108–109

Racism
  by African-Americans, 43–44,
      86–87
  Hurston's experiences of, 8,
      17–18, 60–61
  Jim Crow laws, 8, 22, 88
  as theme, 22, 82–88, 103–104

Seraph on Sewanee, 99–100
sexual abuse, 18–19, 25
slavery
  Nanny's as formative, 18, 24, 40
  oral traditions, 15, 16, 23, 42, 48,
      52–53
  as theme, 63, 75–79, 85–86, 92–94
Sop-de-Bottom, 30, 81
speakerly text, 55
Starks, Joe
  basis for, 52
  character study, 19–20, 28, 32–36
  in Janie's quest, 71–74
  Janie's relationship with, 20–21,
      26–27, 69, 71, 77

motivations of, 69, 77–78
striving of as theme, 86
storytelling, 15, 16, 23, 42, 48, 52–53

Taylor, Johnny, 18, 68
Tell My Horse, 94–96
"The Gilded Six-Bits," 89
Their Eyes Were Watching God
  folk traditions in, 46
  Hurston on, 56, 62
  language style, 51, 54–56, 63–64
  legacy, 101–110
  literary criticisms, 29, 84
  perspective, 17
  plot summary, 15–22
  publishing of, 57, 106
  purpose, 65–66, 103, 104
  reviews, 29, 57, 61–65
  structure, 16, 52–54
  themes (See themes)
  writing of, 13–14
themes
  growth/self-realization, 23–30,
      35–37, 67–74, 101–102
  the horizon, 73–74
  Janie's quest, 70–74
  loneliness, 19–20, 25
  the mule, 75–79
  pear tree, 67–70
  racism as (See racism)
  slavery as (See slavery)
  striving as, 86
  the trial, 22, 29, 79–82, 88
Tompkins, Lucille, 64–65
Turner, Mrs., 43–44, 86–87

Voodoo, 10–13, 47–52, 94–96